The Sandringham Flower Show

WRITTEN BY

ALISON CROOSE

Gardening Consultant
Tim Newbury

Text Copyright © 1999 Alison Croose
This edition copyright © 1999 Eastern Counties Newspaper Group

Published by Eastern Counties Newspaper Group,
Prospect House, Rouen Road, Norwich, Norfolk NR1 1RE.

All rights reserved. No part of this publication may be reproduced, stored in a retrieval system
or transmitted in any form or by any means, electronic, mechanical, photocopying,
recording or otherwise, without the prior permission of the publishers.

ISBN 1902729013

Designed by Richard Snowball

All photographs and illustrations in this book are copyright © ECNG except for:-
Anglia Television (opposite introduction) PA News (pages 10,12) and Jarrold Publishing (pages 15, 20, 28, 29, 72)
All colour photographs have been taken by EDP photographers,
John Hocknell and Brian Waite.

With grateful thanks to Sandringham Estate Cottage Horticultural Society
whose chairman David Reeve has given wholehearted support to this book;
also for all the help provided by many people closely
associated with Sandringham Estate.

The author was able to make use of material from the Royal Archives
with the gracious permission of Her Majesty the Queen.

CLARENCE HOUSE
SW1A 1BA

Whenever I come to Sandringham I am reminded of the words written by King George V: "Dear old Sandringham, the place I love better than anywhere in the world", as I feel the same about the Flower Show. It has always been the highlight of my July visit to Norfolk for it is an event which gives a permanence and stability in the fast-changing world of today.

The familiar faces of many of the exhibitors, some of whom are the children of those who worked on the Estate during and after the War, make me feel at home, and I am always amazed at the high standard of produce and by the marvellous support the Show receives from local people and organisations.

I send to all those associated with the Sandringham Flower Show my best wishes for the future.

ELIZABETH R
Queen Mother

February 1999

Show chairman Fred Waite with rose grower Willem Tysterman, secretary Ernest Francis and president Julian Loyd with the Sandringham Centenary rose bred for the 100th show in 1980.

INTRODUCTION

The basic ingredients of Sandringham Flower Show are no different from hundreds of other village shows the length and breadth of Britain. But the Sandringham show is a phenomenon. It is a national event centred on one much-loved person – Queen Elizabeth the Queen Mother. She first attended the show with King George VI and has never missed the occasion since the war, enjoying the continuity of the event where she renews the acquaintance of people she has known for years.

Like so many other village shows, prized blooms, fruit and vegetables are displayed in marquees - but on the royal estate in Norfolk the tents are put up in parkland within sight of Sandringham House, the Queen's privately-owned country retreat. The entries are modest, the flowers are exhibited in rusty metal vases on trestle tables - but because of the show's close royal associations, the event is the destination of thousands of people from all over Britain and abroad.

The show began soon after Sandringham House became a royal home in 1862 and the 20th century will end with the 118th show. The event has always enjoyed royal patronage and even in its early days attracted big crowds. It has developed through the generations but many of its attractions have remained constant. The show's great charm is that its pleasures are simple and that is no doubt one of the reasons why the last Wednesday in July remains a red-letter day on the Queen Mother's calendar.

A painting of the Prince and Princess of Wales with two of their children, Prince Albert Victor and Princess Maud, later Queen of Norway. The painting, by Heinrich von Angeli, is reproduced by gracious permission of Her Majesty The Queen.

The first Sandringham Flower Show was held just two years after Albert Edward, the Prince of Wales, bought Sandringham House in 1862. It was initially a small, local show until Sandringham Estate Cottage Horticultural Society was established and staged its first show on September 20th 1866.

The society's purpose was to "encourage labourers and others on the Royal Estate in the cultivation of their gardens and allotments, their wives and housekeepers in maintaining neatness and cleanliness in the cottages and the children in improving their needlework and writing".

From the start the show enjoyed the patronage of the Prince of Wales and at the first show the rector of Wolferton and secretary of the society Rev W W Dickinson spoke of the Prince's "ready co-operation in the enterprise".

Mr Dickinson said it was the society's aim to "improve the moral and physical well-being of the labouring classes" and to promote a feeling of mutual good-will between employers and employed.

The Prince of Wales' concern for the welfare of his tenants, though sounding feudal in the language of the 19th century, was to be the start of a long, unique relationship between the Royal Family and the people of West Norfolk.

The Prince of Wales, later to become King Edward VII, was the first of four generations of monarchs who have been able to relax away from the cares of state at their privately-owned country retreat with its delightful woodland, glorious banks of rhododendrons and vast heathland. Like his successors the Prince had a great affection for Sandringham and became closely involved in the life of the estate.

The Prince of Wales was the eldest son of Queen Victoria and the Prince Consort, who married Prince Alexandra of Denmark the year after he took over the estate and its 7000 acres. The couple were at the centre of fashionable society. Their social life ranged from formal visits by heads of state from all over the world to country weekend house parties to which neighbours from other Norfolk estates were among the guests.

The Prince and Princess took a great interest in the design and layout of the gardens around the house. New lakes were created, a large rockery was built, flower beds and a rose garden laid out and a great variety of trees planted. The work occupied 60 gardeners.

The Prince was a racing enthusiast and established both Sandringham and Wolferton stud farms. The whole estate was a busy place requiring a large number of employees so there was a thriving local community to participate in the flower show.

The Prince of Wales was consulted about the organisation of the show and when the horticultural society drew up its set of rules they were submitted for his approval. From the first committee meeting held at the rectory, attended by six members and chaired by the rector, Sandringham Estate Cottage Horticultural Society existed solely to stage the annual show. It has never been run for profit.

The success of the first show held in Sandringham Park was widely publicised. Organisers declared: "There was not a better show to be seen in England".

Even The Times carried a report which was very significant for a very modest village event. It said: "So great an assemblage has not been seen in the neighbourhood of the Prince of Wales' Norfolk seat since the first arrival of the Princess Alexandra to her new home immediately after the auspicious wedding.

Not only were there many thousands of respectable persons permitted to roam through the park, gardens and grounds, but the beautiful little church, and particularly the royal pew, was visited and inspected with considerable interest".

The Times enthusiastically reported that "the potatoes were exceedingly fine", there were "some charming dahlias" and all the exhibitions of the cottagers were "wonderfully good".

At that first show the pattern was established: the crowd of well over 3000 was huge for a village event, the standard of entries was high and the proceeds went to worthy causes. The gardens of the house were opened to the public so the occasion provided the opportunity for people to see the new royal residence and the changes which had been made to the house and grounds.

It was reported that: "The gardens and pleasure grounds were thrown open to visitors and a very great number of all classes from far and wide availed themselves of the much desired opportunity of inspecting the favourite retreat of the Prince and Princess and witnessing the great improvements effected and in progress in every portion of the estate".

In order to "prevent the intrusion of undesirable company" the organising committee "judiciously decided upon charging an admission fee of one shilling to non-members of the society".

To encourage garden cultivation and "promote habits of industry and order among cottagers" prizes were awarded for the good order and condition of gardens and allotments and for the fruit, flowers and vegetables grown. The Prince and Princess of Wales gave special prizes for the best gardens and neatest cottages in the parishes of Sandringham and

The showground in the 1920s.

Babingley, West Newton and Appleton, Wolferton and Dersingham.

Fifty classes attracted a huge entry which delighted the show's organisers. The flowers and fruits were displayed in a 75-foot long tent and the vegetables in another 35 feet long.

There were so many vegetables exhibited that the smaller tent overflowed and tables were set up outside for beans, cauliflowers and gourds. The standard of the potatoes was so high extra prizes were

Historic records - the first minutes of the show committee and schedules of early shows.

awarded. A third tent served refreshments provided by the Globe Hotel of King's Lynn.

That first show was held in September so fruit included apples, pears, plums, grapes and currants. Flowers ranged from roses, dahlias, asters and marigolds to bouquets of wild flowers gathered by schoolchildren. There was a display of exotic plants from Prince Edward's greenhouses and "ingenious floral devices by honorary contributors".

The show lasted from noon until 6pm and

visitors streamed in through the entrance near the church where the gate was decorated with foliage surmounted by a floral crown. As well as the tents of exhibits and displays band music was a feature of the first show where the 1st Norfolk Rifles entertained the crowd.

The show was considered particularly successful in having attracted such a big entry of produce even though it was organised at only three months notice. At the conclusion three cheers were given for the Prince and Princess in appreciation of their concern for "the welfare and pleasure of estate workers".

The first event had a surplus of funds of £57 after prize money had been paid out. From the proceeds £10 was given to West Norfolk and King's Lynn Hospital. Lynn Museum, the National Lifeboat Institution, and the Blind Institution were each given £5. It was decided to spend £4 19s 2d on blankets for parishioners on the estate. The society retained £27.

By 1891 the list of subscribers was growing. Headed by the Prince and Princess of Wales who each contributed five guineas the list included businesses and individuals who gave five or ten shillings. That year the statement of accounts showed that £54 was spent on prizes, £18 on the band and £11 on the hire of tents. The popularity of the flower show guaranteed its future though the date was soon moved forward to July.

Its fame quickly spread way beyond the estate. People at King's Lynn took a holiday and caught excursion trains of 20 carriages crammed with passengers who were ferried by bus and other vehicles to the showground. While the Great Eastern Railway carried passengers from Lynn to Dersingham, the Midland and Great Northern carried 450 to Hillington, including passengers from Cromer, Yarmouth and Norwich.

As the show became well-established additional entertainment was organised. A band remained a popular attraction and more music was added to the programme. Recitals were played in Sandringham Church on the organ given by the Princess of Wales after the Prince recovered from illness in 1872. There were also vocal solos.

By the 1890s another development was the introduction of classes for "tastefully decorated" bicycles, tradesmen's horse or pony and cart and an open class for decorated horse or pony and trap. Competitors took part in a grand parade round the showground.

A report of the 1896 show commented on the effect of the drought. "Potatoes were in splendid condition but the tubers were not so large as usual owing to the drought. Competitors should be a little more careful in preparing potatoes for show as in many instances the skins were rubbed off". Onions were "wonderfully fine" and there were so many good entries extra prizes were awarded. An increasing variety of vegetables were exhibited but the show was held too late in the season for some soft fruits.

In the amateur classes, table decorations were described as "neat and tasteful" and "far in advance of last year, the greatest fault now being that the specimens were a little too high in the centre". Ornamental baskets of flowers and ferns were good "but most of them were overloaded". Success was well-rewarded in the amateur classes where the subscription was three shillings. A first prize of ten shillings was awarded to "amateurs not employing professional gardeners" for the best collection of cut flowers - both hot house and outdoor. There was also a ten shilling first prize for an ornamental basket of flowers and ferns, five shillings for the best three button-hole bouquets and 21 shillings for the best table decoration.

From the early days of the show trade stands added to the colour with displays including roses, sweet peas, godetias and pelargoniums.

Sandringham was King Edward VII's home for 49 years. He made it a glittering centre of society and transformed the shooting into some of the finest in the country.

King George V had known the estate all his life and he spoke of it with great affection, as did King George VI. Their pleasure in spending time at their country retreat included their involvement in all aspects of the life of the estate - and one of the major events of each year was the flower show to which each monarch gave support and patronage.

But Sandringham, like every other community, had to curtail its pleasures in times of international conflict and three major wars resulted in the cancellation of the flower show. In 1920 the event sprang back into life after the first world war when the 49th show was held on July 21 and attracted a record attendance of 6000.

Under the headline "Gala Day at Sandringham" the Eastern Daily Press said the show had been "resuscitated" after six years of war. The report waxed lyrical about the event. "It is not extravagant to suggest that it had a setting and a charm which can scarcely be rivalled by any show of the same proportions in the whole country. What gave it its special claim to popularity and made it such an attractive social function was the fact that it was held in Sandringham Park and within sight of Sandringham House and York Cottage".

As the Royal Family was not in residence "every liberty was offered to the visitors to roam about the grounds pretty well as they pleased". The kitchen gardens, the royal stables and kennels, the ornamental flower beds and lakes plus the show itself provided an enjoyable afternoon outing.

Exhibits in the cottagers' section were judged by Walter Barnes, head gardener to Lord Rocksavage of Houghton Hall and William Barnes, head gardener to Major Bagge of Gaywood Hall.

There was a competition for baskets of six kinds of vegetables among 20 vegetable classes including displays of 20 pods of peas, 12 pods of broad beans or three cabbages. There were classes for four types of potato with each entry consisting of nine potatoes and the winner received ten shillings. Shallots and onions were "extraordinarily good and were the pick of the section". Several extra prizes were awarded for peas which were "excellent and probably the best lot ever seen at the show".

There were 12 classes for cut flowers including a collection of four different kinds of perennials, six kinds of annuals and separate classes for dahlias,

SANDRINGHAM HOUSE GARDENS
The Head Gardener

Martin Woods, Sandringham's head gardener.

Sandringham's head gardener, Martin Woods, has the responsibility of ensuring the 60-acre Gardens around the house are at their peak, as far as the seasons allow, when members of the Royal Family are in residence. That is a considerable challenge as their principle visit is in the depth of winter, at Christmas and New Year. He also has to plan carefully the timing of major or disruptive work.

Mr Woods took over as head gardener in 1996 when his predecessor Fred Waite retired after 27 years in charge of the gardens. Mr Woods had spent 16 years working and training in the Gardens and was prepared for the task by undertaking management courses and gaining qualifications from the Royal Horticultural Society.

The policy in the Gardens is to provide continuity from year to year while allowing the Gardens to develop with the introduction of new plants and ideas so they do not become static museum pieces. It is the head gardener's role to ensure this fine balance is maintained and the relatively informal nature of the layout at Sandringham is helpful in achieving these aims.

Staffing levels contrast markedly with the early years of their development when about 60 staff were employed, compared with the current figure of seven full-time staff plus two students looking after the same area , about seven acres per person. Modern technology is used where possible to make the most efficient use of the reduced labour force, particularly the cutting of lawns and other grass areas.

Mr Woods has developed a policy through which his staff are responsible for, or work within, the same areas of the Gardens as much as possible. This enables

SANDRINGHAM HOUSE GARDENS

Checking for frost damage.

gardeners to become more familiar with all aspects of the areas with which they are involved and they develop greater skills and gain more valuable experience than by being constantly moved around. An example of this policy in practice is the Pleached Lime Avenue which is currently being managed to encourage the development of a higher canopy. It will take several years and is beneficial to both the trees and the gardeners that some sort of continuity is provided.

There used to be many gardeners employed in the walled kitchen garden where it was the head gardener's role to ensure a constant and varied supply of quality vegetables, fruit and flowers for the House all the year round. This responsibility no longer exists since the walled garden declined and became neglected and overgrown. There is a possibility it may be restored but it is more likely to be a smaller scale version of its former glory.

King George V pheasant shooting at Sandringham.

picotees or carnations, roses, stocks, lilies, pansies, sweet williams and sweet peas. There was concern that the classses for cut flowers "lacked uniformity and might in some cases have been shown with more artistic effect". Comment was also made on the paucity of the collections of annuals.

A feature of the show was the section for table decorations which had its own tent and attracted ten entries. The winning entry incorporated penstemon, sweet peas and lavender. The section for bread, jam, eggs and honey was developing and there was a five shilling prize for the best currant cake or jar of gooseberry or blackcurrant jam.

Leading nurserymen from the area had trade stands, Wisbech Town Silver Prize Band provided musical entertainment outside and Sandringham church organist Frederick J Bone gave a recital in the church of St Mary Magdalene. Another tradition had been established - a cricket team representing Sandringham estate played a match against a King's Lynn eleven.

The show went from strength to strength and two years later it seemed that all roads led to Sandringham and another record attendance was achieved as nearly 8000 people converged on the showground from a wide area. There were 1500 entries - double the previous year when a long drought had forced the cancellation of many classes.

Long family associations with the estate are illustrated by some of the surnames featured among the winners of the 1922 show - including Hanslip, Annison, Hipkin and Benstead - which remain familiar names in the Sandringham area.

Such was the prestige of the show that horticulture firms including Sutton and Sons from Reading and Carter and Company from London were among the nurserymen and florists with trade stands.

The success of the show was much appreciated by its royal patrons and after visiting the event on July 30 1924 Queen Alexandra wrote to the chairman of the organising committee, the Rev A R H Grant offering her "cordial congratulations". She had much admired the beautiful exhibits and was particularly glad to notice the keenness of the competition for the cottagers' prizes. The letter said the Queen was "much struck with the excellence of the arrangements which were perfect. The number of people present was surprising and there was absolutely no hitch throughout the day".

Each monarch has not only given patronage to the show but offered practical support to the organisers. In 1914, to encourage more people to compete for the £20 prizes for the best kept cottages and gardens, King George V supported the idea of 50 King's 'Premiums' of five shillings each being offered to the best kept gardens and 50 Queen's 'Premiums' for the best kept among the 250 cottages on the estate. Framed cards were given to the winners. The incentive grew out of concern that there were so few entries that the prizes kept going to the same people. Sandringham agent Frank Beck thought the proposal would generate "very real and friendly rivalry amongst the cottagers which will lead to a great improvement in the state of both cottages

The Duke and Duchess of York soon after their marriage.

Two winners of the challenge cup presented by King George VI - Sidney Hooks and William Warnes whose sons have also won the trophy.

and gardens". The idea developed and eventually illustrated certificates selected by the King were issued.

When King Edward VIII came to the throne in 1936 he gave permission for the show to be held as usual. Soon after King George VI ascended the throne he gave a challenge cup for the best kept garden on the estate - a trophy which is still awarded each year - and which was presented with a certificate headed Buckingham Palace. The King presented the cup to the first winner in 1938 and the gardens competition continued through the war although the show was not held from 1939 until it resumed, with the King's permission, in 1949.

SANDRINGHAM HOUSE GARDENS
Shrubs & Perennials

Dwarf conifers are used to provide winter cover.

The principles for plant selection adopted by the head gardener at Sandringham are the same as for an average garden to give a succession of interest. While trees provide the height, scale and backcloth, smaller-scale planting with perennials - ranging from bulbs and grasses to shrubs including dwarf conifers - provide varying colour and texture throughout the year.

Evergreen shrubs are essential to the success of the Gardens, not only to provide background to smaller plants and valuable screening, but also for their own interest of flower, foliage and fruit. Attractive foliage is clearly beneficial in the winter, and indeed some of the dwarf conifers to be found on the Rockery and above the waterfall actually improve in colour during the cold, darker months including Junipers (*Juniperus x media* Blue and Gold, *J. scopulorum* Skyrocket) and Thuja (*T. occidentalis* Rheingold).

Several examples of the variegated Box (*Buxus sempervirens Elegantissima*) are to be found, especially in the sunny margins of the tree and shrub border to the north of the North Garden. In the Woodland Garden and around the Norwich Gates are several evergreens chosen for their flower interest. Rhododendrons are most notable in this respect, though the R. ponticum found alongside the drive at Sandringham is too vigorous for most ordinary gardens. Camellias are equally noteworthy flowers, requiring similar conditions to Rhododendrons. Scent is a particular bonus and there are several evergreen shrubs with scented, winter flowers which makes them particularly desirable – Mahonia Charity and Osmanthus delavayi Latifolius at the southern end of the Dell, and Azara microphylla at the eastern end of the Woodland Walk and also trained against the walls of the house.

Deciduous shrubs which provide interest at various times of the year are found throughout. Some are well-known such as the Butterfly Bush (*Buddleia davidii*) and Forsythia. Other less common ones include Ribes speciosum with its pendant Fuchsia-like flowers in spring in the Dell, and nearby Decaisnea fargesii with its walnut leaves and curious bright blue pods of beans in autumn. Not all the deciduous shrubs are selected purely for their flower, though. Some, such as Parrotia persica in the Woodland Walk are grown just for their autumn colour, while just to the west of this, the Smoke Bush (*Cotinus coggygria* Royal Purple) is grown for its brilliant deep purple foliage as well as its hazy flowers in summer.

Winter stem colour plays a vital role here, as in all gardens. Dogwood (*Cornus alba Sibirica*) is planted to catch the low winter sun by the upper lake where it thrives in the heavier soil, and is cut back regularly to produce bright red stems at leaf fall. Perennials are used in a number of ways – some in drifts of different varieties along the Stream Walk and particularly by the lakes. Others are interplanted among and in front of taller shrubs to create a balance of height. With few exceptions, though, perennials found in the gardens have been selected not only for their flowers but also for their general reliability and usefulness as ground cover.

Plants falling into this category include Lady's Mantle (*Alchemilla mollis*), Hosta in variety, Day Lilies (*Hemerocallis spp.*), Hardy Geraniums (*Geranium spp.*), Siberian Iris (*Iris sibirica* Ottawa) and Epimedium perralderianum. Extending the period of flowering interest into late winter and early spring, bulbs such as Daffodils (*Narcissus*), Snowdrops (*Galanthus*) and Winter Aconite (*Eranthis*) are planted in large drifts to naturalise either within lawn areas and around the bases of individual trees, or as underplantings, particularly within the Woodland Walk where Bluebells are very striking in late spring.

Rhododendrons and Azaleas border the lawn.

Mary Relph (right of picture) photographs the Queen Mother at the 1952 show.

Ever since Mary Relph was a young girl and discovered the existence of the Royal Family she has been an enthusiastic royal-watcher.

"I was fascinated by them, collected pictures of them and as children we used to play kings and queens. I wore a cardboard crown and turned a blue bedspread into a cape," she says.

Mrs Relph grew up in the West Norfolk village of Shouldham where her family operated Matthews Coaches which ran excursions to the flower show. "I always used to go with my mother and sister and we would line up to see the Queen Mother who was the centre of attention. That was the big attraction for me," says Mrs Relph. "The Queen Mother always spoke to people. She has always been very charming

Years later Mary Relph shows the photograph opposite to the Queen Mother.

Mary Relph gives flowers to the Queen Mother.

During the 1950s, Princess Margaret joined her mother at the show.

and has time for everyone, young and old."

Mrs Relph has rarely missed the event and Sandringham Flower Show remains one of her favourite days of the year - especially since the Prince of Wales has also become a regular visitor. "I love every minute of it. I'm a big fan of the Queen Mother and I'm a great admirer of Prince Charles."

She says the basic appeal of the event as a simple flower show has changed little over the years although it is now run on a much bigger scale with dozens of charity stalls. "It has always been a big social event, a treat for families with a nice atmosphere." Security has been stepped up since the early post-war days. "There were no ropes for the crowd to stand behind. The Queen Mother would just walk around freely. The public didn't present her with flowers in those days," Mrs Relph says.

But in the 1980s and 1990s royal watchers from all over country have vied for the best vantage points where they will have a good chance of presenting flowers and having a chat with the royal visitors. So Mrs Relph arrives at the show at 6.45am to claim a prime spot just outside the flower tent where she is prepared to wait for more than four hours for the spectacle she loves - the arrival of the Queen Mother and the Prince of Wales in a horse-drawn open carriage.

If all goes well she presents a bunch of flowers to the Queen Mother and on one occasion Mrs Relph was able to show the Queen Mother her photograph of the 1952 event when, as a teenager, she was pictured with her camera poised to record the occasion. "The Queen Mother, and the Prince of Wales, were both very interested to see it," she says.

After watching the Queen Mother go into the flower marquees Mrs Relph dashes across the showground to another vantage point to see the Royal visitors conclude their tour. She has hundreds of photographs of the show over the years. Once when the Duke and Duchess of Kent and their children attended she asked the Duchess if she could take her photograph. The Duchess's friendly response was immediate: "Yes, please do."

SANDRINGHAM HOUSE GARDENS
Water

A view of the Stream Walk.

Water is an integral part of the grounds of Sandringham House, and principally takes the form of two lakes to the south of the West Lawns. These lakes were created at the request of Edward Prince of Wales and Princess Alexandra toward the end of the 19th century. The upper one which is at a higher level, is fed by a natural spring at its western end whilst the lower lake, further to the south, is supplied by a stream running into its eastern arm adjacent to York Cottage. Whilst the lakes are artificial in the sense that they were specially excavated, great care was taken to ensure that they not only fitted into the existing landscape but that they added additional qualities to the grounds by enhancing views and creating wet areas for planting.

To accommodate and emphasise the changes in level, a large rockery was created on the east side of the upper lake, into which was built a small boathouse. Some of the rock is of the locally occurring sandstone, but the larger pieces which form the dramatic outcrop over and around the boathouse are actually artificial and are known as "Pulhamite" after the man who invented them, James Pulham. By a process of fusion and moulding he was able to combine natural aggregate with clay to form 'rocks' or stone which after years of weathering are virtually indistinguishable from the real thing. The beauty of his system was that he could tailor pieces of stone to exactly match the dimensions and texture he required. Although the scale of this rockery is not comparable with today's small private gardens, the same principles of rockery-building still apply. The rock outcrops are layered and the strata lines are parallel to each other as would be found naturally. At the head of the lower lake, a waterfall fed from the upper lake was constructed from Pulhamite at the same time.

The magnitude of these pieces of rockwork meant that popular alpine plants such as Aubrieta, Dianthus deltoides and Arabis would have been completely inappropriate because of their small size. Instead, larger scale plants were used, particularly dwarf and slow-growing conifers including Juniperus squamata Meyeri, Chamaecyparis lawsoniana Columnaris and Chamaecyparis lawsoniana Minima Aurea, as well as shrubs such as the unusual Euryops pectinatus with its silvery leaves and bright yellow flowers in May or June and Japanese Maples (*Acer palmatum spp.*).

The margins of the northern end and the narrow western arm of the upper lake are rich in plants which thrive in the moist, heavy soil. These include traditional varieties of Hosta, Astilbe and Iris – especially Iris pseudacorus or Yellow Flag Iris which grows right into the shallow water – as well as some very elegant hardy ferns such as the Shuttlecock Fern (*Mateuccia struthiopteris*) and appropriately the Royal Fern (*Osmunda regalis*) which sprouts out of the top of curious, dark 'termite mounds' of dead stalk bases.

On either side of the narrow inlet spring are two standard Wisterias which when in flower (frosts permitting) in late April and early May, form a delightful framed view of the summerhouse or 'Nest' on top of the distant rockery. More marginal and moisture-loving plants are to be found along the wet ditch and stream which enter the Gardens on the east side near the road boundary and make their way through the Stream Walk to join the lower lake. As well as Hostas, Astilbe, Rodgersia, Primula and other well-known bog plants, there are less common but equally attractive varieties such as Kirengeshoma palmata with its tall leafy stems and pendulous creamy yellow flowers in late summer, and Lysichiton americanum or Skunk Cabbage whose rather dubious scent is more than offset by its massive yellow flowering spathes in mid to late spring. Possibly the most striking feature in summer, is a huge drift of Gunnera (*G. manicata*) with its massive umbrella-sized bristly leaves and strange upright flower spikes.

The upper lake in spring.

The great charm of Sandringham Flower Show is its timeless quality. There have been changes over the years but none has affected the dignified way the show has maintained its appeal without becoming overly influenced by populist forms of entertainment. It is a village show at heart organised by people who live and work on the royal estate and strive to ensure the show's standards are maintained. They resist commercialisation and are particular about the organisations and individuals who have stalls around the showground.

The aim is to give visitors a good day out and at the same time raise funds for charities. The society only retains enough money to meet the costs of staging the next show and the balance of the proceeds go to organisations mainly in West Norfolk. More than £200,000 has been distributed in the past 18 years to causes such as West Norfolk Home Hospice Support Group, St John Ambulance, the Break Home at Hunstanton, Victim Support at King's Lynn, and the Leonard Cheshire Foundation which runs Park House hotel for the disabled at Sandringham, converted from the birthplace and childhood home of Diana, Princess of Wales.

Throughout its history the show has enjoyed royal patronage which has given it huge prestige and made it nationally famous. But Sandringham does not try to emulate the Chelsea Flower Show and much of its appeal lies in its lack of pretension. In the giant

A coach and horses from the Royal Mews at Buckingham Palace at the show.

Admiring the blooms in the flower tent.

marquees, entries in the flower, fruit and vegetable classes are displayed on simple trestle tables and blooms are shown in green metal vases which appear to have seen better days. Former show chairman Fred Waite remembers a delightful back-handed compliment he received from a regular visitor who said: "I like coming here because you are 25 years behind the times."

Organisers try to foster a friendly atmosphere and are rewarded with numerous words of praise. One particularly appropriate and welcoming gesture is to have multi-lingual announcements made over the loud-speakers as there are always many foreign visitors among the crowd which averages 16,000. Each year about 100 coaches from all over the country run special trips taking hundreds of people to the show. Holidaymakers staying in Norfolk - including caravanners and campers from the two sites on the royal estate – arrange their visits to coincide with the show which is always well-supported by people living in East Anglia.

On the last Wednesday in July - a day which is more often than not blessed with fine, sunny weather - coaches which left the Midlands and southern England at dawn arrive on the estate as the car parks fill up. Spectators line up behind the ropes around the large grassed area outside the flower marquees which provide the setting for the start of the royal visit, and for most people the

Meeting the committee.

arrival of the Queen Mother signals the opening of the event.

In terms of royal protocol her attendance at the show is regarded as a private visit rather than an official engagement so no formal announcement is made in advance of the day. But there is no doubt that the date is one of the first to be marked in the Queen Mother's diary each year. For years her annual routine has been to spend the last week of July at Sandringham House - which is closed to visitors for the period of her stay - so that her summer break in West Norfolk coincides with the flower show and with King's Lynn Festival of which she is patron.

When she broke her hip in a fall at Sandringham Stud in January 1998 and was taken to a London hospital for a hip-replacement operation she left Norfolk with the words: "I'll be back for the flower show." And she was. Although she never misses the show she treats each occasion like a new adventure, eager to see and hear about the entries and how they have been affected by the weather, and to find out if there have been any innovations or changes in the show's format.

Most of all she likes to meet the people. The Queen Mother's affection for the Sandringham estate embraces the people who live and work there and she delights in seeing lots of familiar faces, in renewing acquaintances and catching up on their news. Hers is a very genuine interest because she knows the second and third generations of families whom she met when King George VI first took her to Sandringham after their marriage in 1923. For her beloved 'Bertie' Sandringham was 'home'. It was where he was born and was the place where his father, King George V,

Making friends.

was happiest and it clearly has a special place in the Queen Mother's heart.

So the flower show, the only event organised by and for people who live and work on the estate, is a highlight of the year for them and for her. The Queen Mother has frequently been accompanied by other members of the Royal Family. The Queen, like the Queen Mother, is patron of the show and has attended twice but it is recognised that it is the Queen Mother's day. The Duke and Duchess of Kent and their young family were also regular visitors during the 1970s and 1980s when they lived at Anmer Hall on the Sandringham estate.

In 1958 the Prince of Wales and Princess Anne delighted the crowd when they joined the Queen Mother at the show after travelling by train from

The Prince of Wales with choreographer Sir Frederick Ashton.

Ruth Lady Fermoy, the Queen Mother's close friend and lady-in-waiting.

London to Wolferton station. The youngsters ran up to their grandmother and threw their arms round her neck and greeted her with an affectionate kiss. The Prince and Princess showed particular interest in the game birds and pigeons in the fur and feather tent and watched a class of rabbits being judged.

Prince Charles' visit to Norfolk came just a few days after it was announced that he was to take the title Prince of Wales. It is believed he was the first Prince of Wales to visit the flower show since Prince Edward, later King Edward VII, promoted the first show in Sandringham Park in 1866. Since 1988 the Prince of Wales has joined his grandmother and obviously enjoys letting her take centre stage and is happy to be out of the official limelight though he always gets a very warm welcome from the crowd.

The Queen Mother invites close friends, especially those associated with the world of music and the arts, to join her at Sandringham during the week of the show. For many years Ruth, Lady Fermoy, the Queen Mother's close friend and lady-in-waiting and maternal grandmother to Diana, Princess of Wales, was always at her side. Personalities such as ballet dancer and choreographer Sir Frederick Ashton and Sir Hugh Casson, former president of the Royal Academy, entered into the

The Prince of Wales meets the bandmaster.

spirit of the show and gathered ideas for their own gardens. The Duke and Duchess of Grafton, former chairman of the Arts Council the Earl Gowrie and the Countess, conductor Raymond Leppard, artists Derek Hill and Edward Seago, have been regular visitors as were Lord David Cecil and Lady Cecil in the 1960 and 1970s.

An air of eager anticipation builds up from 10am on show day as officials bustle in and out of the committee tent carrying out last minute tasks. Anxious eyes look skyward if there is any chance of rain but mostly it is a day for summer frocks and light-weight suits for those involved with the running of the show and more casual wear for crowds standing up to 10 deep along the route taken by the royal party.

Major bands have remained popular attractions. The bands of the Coldstream Guards, the Royal Marines, the Welsh Guards, the Queen's Dragoon

SANDRINGHAM HOUSE GARDENS
Wildlife

The Woodland Walk – a haven for wild life.

Within the 60 acres of gardens around Sandringham House, there are few, if any, areas which could be truly called wild as the whole Estate is subject to the influence of man. But there is a noticeable variety of wildlife within the Gardens, even in those parts which are entirely composed of 'alien' ornamental plants. One of the factors contributing to this variety is the very low usage of chemicals, particularly herbicides and insecticides which allows a larger and more varied insect population to develop. That in turn provides food, particularly at nesting time, for many insectivorous birds including blackbirds, tits and wrens, as well as more unusual species such as goldcrests and flycatchers.

A 'tidy–up' policy which is commonly found in many public parks and open spaces is only enforced at Sandringham for reasons of safety or in selected areas where it is felt to be most appropriate. Fallen trees in woodland areas are left to gradually rot back into the soil, again boosting the insect population – including the earthworms that hedgehogs favour – and providing ideal growing and breeding conditions for dozens of native fungi. Dead trees, if safe, can be left as potential homes and larders for grub-eating birds like woodpeckers.

Fallen leaves of both deciduous broadleaved trees such as Oak, Beech and evergreen conifers with needles (Pine, Spruce and Fir) are sometimes left where they land to form a natural mulch and organic soil improver, or else they are raked up from formal lawn areas and redistributed elsewhere in the gardens as a mulch or to be composted down for adding to newly cultivated ground. The vast majority of planting in the gardens is informal and almost without exception during the height of the growing season there is little bare soil to be seen due to the canopy of plants whether they are ground–hugging mats of Periwinkle (*Vinca minor*) or large stately masses of evergreen Mahonia Charity. This style of close, ground–cover planting can be mimicked in any size of garden, and provides excellent cover for insects, birds and mammals to move around un–noticed, and for feeding and breeding.

There are many plants within the grounds which also directly provide food for wildlife. A small bed of winter-flowering Heathers (*Erica carnea spp.*) just above the upper lake provides valuable pollen and nectar in late winter and early spring for the first bees, as do Mahonia and Osmanthus in the Dell. In the Woodland Walk, a clearing which receives plenty of sun has been planted with several varieties of Lavender (*Lavandula spp.*). As well as providing an opportunity for visitors to compare the different habits, colour and scent of the various forms on display, the bed also provides food during the summer for hundreds of bees, butterflies and other insects.

Many other spring and summer-flowering plants found in the gardens also provide insects with food in this way including Buddleia, Wisteria, shrub Roses, deciduous Azaleas, Meadowsweet (*Filipendula ulmaria*) and Bluebells. Trees and shrubs which provide fruits, seeds and berries in the autumn and winter are found throughout the Gardens. Although Beech (*Fagus sylvatica*) only produces meaningful seeds or 'mast' about every seven years, other trees such as Oak (*Quercus robur*) are more reliable. In the Woodland Walk, Cotoneaster frigidus produces copious amounts of red berries, while along the sunny margins of this and other borders, shrub Roses such as Rosa rugosa generate large, fleshy hips. There is good news for fruit-eating larger birds like blackbirds and migrant fieldfares with the development of a long holly hedge along the boundary between the Gardens and Sandringham Park.

Spring bulbs provide essential food for insects.

The Queen Mother's outfits always add a splash of colour to the scene.

Guards, the King's Own Border Regiment and the RAF College have all given a musical welcome to the Royal visitors. They add vivid colour to the scene as they march to their allotted space. At 11 o'clock there is an expectant hush, a large posse of regional and national press and television photographers have their cameras poised as all heads crane to catch a first glimpse of the star of the show.

Through the 1990s the Queen Mother arrived with the Prince of Wales in a horse-drawn open carriage as a change from the previous custom of travelling from Sandringham House in a Royal limousine. The appearance of a gleaming Victoria carriage drawn by two grey horses with scarlet uniformed liverymen presents a wonderful spectacle. In 1967 the Queen Mother travelled on one of the open carriages from the Royal Mews at Buckingham Palace which gave displays at the show.

The Queen Mother always adds a splash of colour to the scene. Her dresses and matching loose-fitting coats are often in shades of blue but sometimes in sunshine yellow or pale turquoise. Every outfit is topped with one of her trademark brimmed and veiled hats often decorated at the back with a flower or bow. The Queen Mother makes few concessions to her age – and that includes her footwear. She still favours three-inch high heels, even to walk on the uneven grass of the showground.

First to greet the visitors is the show's president, traditionally the Queen's agent at Sandringham. In the post-war years that was Captain William Fellowes, succeeded in 1964 by Julian Loyd who was knighted with a personal honour from the Queen after his retirement in 1991. He was followed by John Major who was agent until Marcus O'Lone took over in 1998.

After the official welcome, the showground falls silent for the National Anthem played by the visiting band after which the show's chairman leads the Queen Mother along a line-up of show committee members. Charlie Cook was head gardener and chairman of the organising committee for many years. His successor as head gardener, Horace Parsons, took over as chairman in 1964 and Fred Waite was chairman from 1970 for 27 years.

Because of the size of the committee a third of its members - many of them estate employees - are formally presented each year. The Queen Mother knows them all and has the first of many friendly chats of the day.

The line-up includes the latest winner of the cottagers' garden competition to whom the Queen Mother always likes to talk as well as offering a special word of encouragement. She has maintained a close interest in the affable rivalry which has existed between successive generations of several families living on the estate who, over the years, have vied for the challenge cup given by King George VI in 1938, plus the prize, which is now £50.

Police officers ferry flowers in trugs.

The pattern for the Queen Mother's visit is set as she walks the short distance from the welcoming committee line-up into the flower tent. The Queen Mother is cheered and given the first of dozens of bunches of flowers which she will receive in the next 90 minutes. Because the show falls just a few days before her birthday on August 4 she is always presented with numerous early birthday greetings, cards and presents. Gifts come in all shapes and sizes from brightly-crayoned birthday cards made by children to immaculate arrangements of flowers in baskets. If posies have a home-grown look the Queen Mother inevitably asks whether they were picked from the donor's garden. If they were she is clearly delighted and receives them with particular enthusiasm.

Within minutes the Queen Mother's arms are full and she has to pass the flowers on to her lady-in-waiting. Often the gifts are presented so thick and fast that members of her party help carry the load. Police soon became wise to the needs of the occasion and officers use trugs to ferry all the flowers to the royal cars.

The phenomenon of giving flowers in the latter part of the century for all sorts of occasions, both happy and sad, was not a feature of earlier shows when the crowd demonstrated their affection more with cheers and applause. Another contrasting feature of the crowds in recent years has been the greater prominence of cameras. Many people's sight of the Queen Mother is through the view-finder and securing their own photographs of her seems to be their priority.

The flower show itself changes very little from year to year and for everyone involved - including the Queen Mother - the familiar pattern of each event is endearing. Apart from world wars the only year the show was cancelled was in 1981 when the date clashed with the wedding of the Prince of Wales and Lady Diana Spencer. Organisers knew the absence of the Queen Mother would hit attendance figures hard, apart from the fact that most people would be glued to their televisions - so it was decided to cancel the show a year after it had celebrated its centenary.

Subtle changes were observed over the years by officials such as Ron Tilson, a retired Barclays Bank manager, who did the money count for 50 years. He says that immediately after the war when people still enjoyed simple pleasures and there were few events on that scale, the show had a significant place in Norfolk's social calendar. Attendance was especially high when the show resumed after the war, peaking in 1952 following the death of King George VI when 20,000 saw the Queen Mother who was still in mourning.

Mr Tilson remembers well that at least 100 coaches would transport visitors who paid an entrance fee of 2s 6d and gatekeepers worked from 9am-4pm. In those days one tent was devoted to the Queen's Carving School which operated on the estate for many years in former stables now housing a museum. Queen Alexandra founded the school in 1889. Initially boys were taught cabinet-making when they left school. Subsequently Queen Mary took over the school and provided work for disabled soldiers whose homes were on the estate. When it became a school again it was managed by one of the disabled soldiers, Horry Woodhouse. He showed the Queen Mother the work of the boy apprentices and in 1956 she bought a walnut sofa table made by Michael Watt who had speech and hearing difficulties. The school closed in 1957.

Mr Tilson says that in the post-war years many people had allotments and grew fruit and vegetables which they proudly exhibited in classes hotly contested by cottagers living on the estate.

Ernest Francis first knew the flower show as a police constable working on the estate and later became superintendent in charge of the Sandringham police division and member of the show committee. After he retired from the police Mr Francis was secretary and treasurer of the show for 17 years. "It has always been a big day in the life of West Norfolk and after the war it became a national event with bus loads of people coming from all over the country," he says.

"We always tried to get very good nurserymen to have stands to extend the interest and we developed the entertainment side of the show, especially for children, so we could give people an excellent day out. We tried to maintain the standard of all aspects of the show and the dignity of the event." Bigger flower tents were necessary as the number of entries increased. Open classes for floral art have grown considerably. "People from London come to exhibit because they want a prize card with Sandringham on it. Everyone treasures prize cards won at Sandringham."

Mr Francis has also been a keen competitor who won the award for the most points gained by an amateur gardener with his flowers including roses, gladioli and phlox. He sees the show as a social event important to both residents of the estate and to the wider community.

He has special memories of the centenary show in 1980 when Wisbech rose grower Willem Tysterman bred a special hybrid tea rose 'Sandringham Centenary' which was deep salmon pink, for the occasion. "The Queen Mother always asked searching questions and I knew she would be very interested in the new rose and would want to know how it was bred." So he ensured he was well-briefed on the development of the rose - and sure enough his research was fully justified! "She is an extraordinary lady," Mr Francis says.

Sir Julian Loyd, who was agent at Sandringham for 28 years, says the show followed a well-established pattern. "Everything revolves round the Queen Mother's visit. It is definitely her day."

Sir Julian actively encouraged invitations to military bands. Not only did they maintain the tradition established by the first shows where a band was a major attraction but visits by distinguished bands such as the Coldstream Guards and the Royal Marines added considerable kudos to the event. There was one slightly embarrassing occasion when the Royal Marines' coach driver became lost on the way to Norfolk and was unable to get the band to Sandringham in time to give the royal visitors a musical welcome.

Sir Julian says one alteration to the royal visit was

made during his presidency. Originally all members of the show committee were presented to the Queen Mother. But the group was extended to include tenants and others closely associated with the estate so with a larger committee it was decided one third should be in the line-up each year.

When the Queen joined her mother at the show in 1974 it was a very wet day so everyone was sheltering under umbrellas and no-one realised the Queen was there because they were not expecting her. The Queen Mother ensures that rain does not spoil the enjoyment of crowds who she knows expect to see her. So in wet weather she puts a cape over her colourful outfit and uses a transparent umbrella so she can see everyone and they can still see her.

The Queen, dressed for the wet weather, had to shelter under a brolly at the 1974 show.

The Queen Mother uses a transparent umbrella so spectators can still see her.

Royal Walkabouts.

COTTAGE GARDENERS

David Biggs can remember nearly half a century of flower shows since he was a five-year-old and made a papier mâché monster for the school tent where it went on show with handwriting, art, embroidery and needlework. When he was a little older he entered his rabbits and guinea pigs in the fur and feather section and went on to exhibit in all the cottagers' classes and to win the cottagers' gardens competition ten times and the award for winning the most points in the cottagers' classes.

The show has been a central part of his life and though he was never able to realise a much-cherished ambition to earn his living as a gardener - he became an electrician - he notched up a very successful record at the show. He believes the standard in the cottagers' classes is consistently high because of the good practice passed on through generations of estate workers. "We were taught by our fathers how to exhibit," he says.

Mr Biggs' great-grandfather was a gardener for King George V and Queen Mary and his father was a keen exhibitor. David Biggs moved into his home at West Newton 30 years ago, worked hard to create a traditional cottage garden, entered the next show and the garden was judged the best in Sandringham and West Newton. "As points were awarded for vegetables ready for the table at the time of judging it was necessary to have a double planting so there were also vegetables ready for the show a month after the gardens were judged. You had to have a full range of fruits in the garden so I grew grapes, figs, cherries and apricots as well as soft fruit, apples, pears and plums."

"I used to enter 60 exhibits in all the vegetable, fruit, flower, cooking and flower arangement classes. The only thing I didn't enter was eggs because I didn't have any fowl." He managed his success without a greenhouse and reared young plants under cloches and on window ledges in his home. "I had always been encouraged to garden and cook but it meant that at the show I was in competition with my father and his vegetables and my mother's flowers and baking." He had to use a van to ferry all his exhibits to the show including his cakes, jam tarts, lemon curd and wine.

He has not entered for 11 years since sustaining a spinal injury but continues to be a member of the show committee and stewards the judging. "It is still a wonderful day out. It has not altered, we still have a good band and good entertainment in the main ring. The whole beauty of the show is that it has not changed much."

Ann Biggs still has a cross-stitch cushion she made for the schools tent when she was a youngster.

The "monster" her husband David made when he was five.

COTTAGE GARDENERS

David Biggs in his cottage garden.

COTTAGE GARDENERS

John Hannant describes as "my proudest moment" when he was presented to the Queen Mother as joint winner of the cottagers' gardens competition. The certificate from Buckingham Palace declaring his success in 1993 takes pride of place in his albums of mementoes cataloguing his entries and wins in the Sandringham Show. "It's like the Chelsea of West Norfolk and has a lot of prestige round here. It is also the social event of the year for many people," Mr Hannant said.

He and his wife Doreen are eligible to enter the cottagers' classes because they live in an estate property at Dersingham. They were already entering vegetables and flowers in horticultural shows at Dersingham and neighbouring villages when they were urged to exhibit at Sandringham. Soon they were smitten. Mr and Mrs Hannant's lives now revolve round preparing for the Sandringham Show. In the depths of winter they study seed catalogues and Mr Hannant always sows his onion seed in one of his four greenhouses on Boxing Day.

"We don't have a holiday but take time off from work to prepare for the show," says Mrs Hannant who works part-time at the Feathers Hotel at Dersingham. Her husband is gardener and groundsman at Park House Hotel for the disabled, the birthplace and childhood home of Diana, Princess of Wales. "We don't need to go away because the garden is our hobby and we enjoy it," Mrs Hannant adds.

They believe competition is healthy. "This business of showing is having the courage to have a go. You can learn a lot by entering and it helps you improve," Mr Hannant says. "You might not get anywhere at first, then you get a third and you feel you are on the way." Their team effort includes keeping a diary recording every step of their preparations for the show for which there are two key dates. First they have to be ready for the judging of their garden at the end of June and then they work towards the specific entries for the show itself.

Mr Hannant is one of a small, dedicated group of gardeners who enter a tray of nine vegetables (beetroot, cauliflowers, cucumbers, leeks, onions, parsnips, potatoes, runner beans and tomatoes). Among the many wins they have notched up, he has won the cup awarded in the vegetable classes and his wife has won the Prince of Wales trophy in the flower classes. She enters classes for cut flowers, pot plants - including fuchsias and geraniums - and floral art and has competed in the bakery and preserves section. They have so many exhibits to transport to the showground on the eve of the event they have to hire a van to carry them all.

COTTAGE GARDENERS

John and Doreen Hannant tend their cottage garden.

Friendly rivalry between Neville Warnes and John and Doreen Hannant.

COTTAGE GARDENERS

Neville Warnes learned many of his gardening skills from his father but against tough competition, it took 38 attempts before he was awarded the coveted cottagers' gardens trophy. Having found the secret of success Mr Warnes won five years in succession - one of those a joint win with John Hannant. Mr Warnes keeps a very traditional cottage garden surrounding his semi-detached carrstone home at Anmer. It was in the same village that his father William nurtured his garden and became the first person to win the King George VI Cup for four years in succession. In recognition of this achievement in the early 1950s he was given a silver replica of the trophy.

"My father once told me he would liked to have made gardening his profession. He liked it and was good and I think a bit of it rubbed off," says Mr Warnes, a retired farmworker. "I used to help him dig his huge garden. We even used to go out on moonlight nights and work in the garden. I think I prepare vegetables for showing in virtually the same way as my father did."

When Neville Warnes married Pam Hooks in 1953 he was marrying into another Anmer gardening family for his father-in-law Sid Hooks also won the gardens trophy several times. His brother-in-law Bertie Hooks was another winner. Mr Warnes immediately started entering his own garden as well as his vegetables and fruit and flowers and over the years has had dozens of successes. "It was a long while before I won the gardens competition in 1993," he says. "I don't garden specially for the show but I try and keep us self-sufficient in vegetables nearly all the year."

Mr Warnes says it was necessary to rotate crops, especially potatoes and peas, and that was difficult in a small garden where features like his fruit pen, shrubs and herbaceous border had to remain static.

Mr Warnes enters trays of six vegetables - he finds nine too many from a small garden. Like most gardeners Mr Warnes as his own rituals - such as planting runner beans in pots in the third week in April and putting them out the third week in May leaving only a week when he may have to protect them against frost. "I hope to see beans just forming on my birthday on July 9 then I know I shall have beans to show at the end of that month," he says. Mrs Warnes grades fruit for showing and has to find 20 perfect raspberries, 20 red, yellow or green gooseberries and a pint of red, white or black currants.

Mr Warnes says: "Mine is a typical cottage garden - nothing fancy. I grow climbing roses up old iron fence posts and sheep nets. I enjoy growing carnations and roses and have a good collection of phlox. I like all aspects of gardening, nothing is a chore."

COTTAGE GARDENERS

Neville Warnes tends his prize-winning cottage garden and works in his greenhouse.

Neville and Pam Warnes with their trophies.

COTTAGE GARDENERS

When Bert Hooks started exhibiting at Sandringham Flower Show in the early 1950s competition was especially tough among the many talented gardeners on the royal estate. His first attempt in the fruit and vegetable classes with four exhibits did not meet with any success. "I took notice why other people got prizes and I did not," he says. Soon he started picking up class prizes and his large garden at Anmer was awarded the King George VI Challenge Cup for winning the cottagers' gardens competition. Mr Hooks believes judges wanted to see "a real garden, not a showplace."

One of Mr Hooks' greatest rivals was his father, Sid. "It was friendly rivalry but he wouldn't give me a cutting or a potato and my biggest thrill when I did win the gardens competition was beating my father." Mr Hooks senior collected many prizes for his vegetables and his son has enjoyed similar success. Until Bert Hooks retired another of his friendly rivals was his brother-in-law and neighbour at Anmer, Neville Warnes.

Mr Hooks, who worked as farm foreman for a tenant farmer at Anmer, took up the challenge of producing a tray of nine vegetables which soon starting winning prizes. He planted his vegetables with the aim of their being ready for the show though the weather often intervened. But his efforts always ensured the family was self-sufficient in vegetables throughout the year.

He shares his hobby with his wife June who has also entered the bakery and preserves section. "I used to do the heavy work and June trimmed the hedges and did the borders. Roses are my favourite flowers but I also like growing sweet peas and we also entered pot plants," he says.

During the weekend before the show gardeners start preparing their vegetables. But first they have to find nine potatoes of uniform size without any blemishes. They need six onions, 12 pods of peas and 12 pods of broad beans. If a gardener enters a collection of vegetables and a trug of mixed vegetables they would need three dozen top specimens of each kind which is quite a challenge for a cottage gardener with possibly only space for one row of each kind of vegetable. "I would be up before the birds to get everything ready but it is nice that the Queen Mother always spends a lot of time looking at the vegetables," Mr Hooks says.

The Queen Mother chats with Bert Hooks in the line-up of committee members.

COTTAGE GARDENERS

Bert Hooks tends his roses (left), and enjoyed his prize-winning cottage garden in earlier days (top right).

The Queen talks to Bert Hooks in 1984, one of the years he won the cottagers' garden class.

COTTAGE GARDENERS

Diana Fitt-Savage discovered a competitive edge to her character when she starting exhibiting at the flower show after moving to the royal estate in the late 1960s. "It's a lot of work and every year I say I won't take part again but just before the show people ask me what I will be entering. If no-one entered there wouldn't be anything for visitors to see. We do it for fun and I like to support the event because it is part of the estate," says Mrs Fitt-Savage whose husband Tony is organist at Sandringham Church.

She believes that taking part in the flower show started her competitiveness for entering her chihuahuas in dog shows - and their successes have earned her a world-wide reputation in the dog-breeding world. In the section for bakery and preserves Mrs Fitt-Savage enjoys the challenge of getting the best results from a particular recipe. Fruit cakes and sponges are her forte and she has won the cup for most points in the bakery and preserves section. When there was a class for novelty cakes she produced a cottage and garden one year and another intricate entry was a cake in the form of a chrysanthemum.

Her kitchen is a hive of activity on the day before the show as she makes batches of cheese scones, sausage rolls and jam tarts so she has enough to select five good examples of each. When it comes to making a sponge cake - the recipe has recently been changed to a Victoria sandwich - Mrs Fitt-Savage believes the secret of success is large, fresh eggs. "I use the biggest, freshest eggs I can find and beat them like mad. The secret is the selection of the eggs, the beating of them and how the sugar and flour are introduced. That makes all the difference. Getting them out of the tin without their sticking is always a tricky business but my family look forward to eating the failures!" she says. Lemon curd has been another favourite. "It was arduous and time-consuming to make but delicious."

Mrs Fitt-Savage has also enjoyed many successes with her flowers and pot plants but is very philosophical about her entries. "I grow a lot of dahlias outdoors but I don't cosset them. For the basket of flowers I go round the garden and see what I can find. It is the same with pot plants - I grow to please me and hope my tender care will give me something good to enter on the day." Geraniums, fuchsias and African violets are among her specialities.

She welcomes the variety of interest and entertainment the show offers. "It is like a small agricultural show but is very friendly and a social event for many people."

COTTAGE GARDENERS

Diana Fitt-Savage tends her pot plants (left).
Large fresh eggs are the secret of the success of Mrs Fitt-Savage's baking.

A novelty cake in the shape of a chrysanthemum.

get the chance to exchange a few words with their royal favourite. Fellow pensioners are often quite overcome with joy at coming face-to-face with the person who has been the much-loved central figure in the Royal Family for so many years.

But when Mr Waite took his first job at a garden centre at Shrewsbury he never dreamed that he would escort the Queen Mother round Sandringham Flower Show. He worked at the garden centre run by Percy Thrower, the first 'media' gardener, who told him: "Two years at Sandringham would do you good." Percy Thrower arranged with his father-in-law, Charlie Cook, then head gardener at Sandringham, for Mr Waite to join the team of more than 30 gardeners who worked on the royal estate in 1948.

One man who has appreciated as much as anyone the Queen Mother's very special affection for Sandringham and its flower show is Fred Waite who, as chairman, escorted her round the show for 27 years. He has witnessed at close range her absolute pleasure in her annual visit to the show where she loves to see so many familiar faces and revels in the customary informality of the occasion. "I'm sure the show is one of the first things put in her diary each year. She enjoys gardens and is interested in nature," he says.

He is also acutely aware of the delight of spectators, especially those of the Queen Mother's generation, when they

For 27 years show chairman Fred Waite escorted the Queen Mother round the show.

The Queen Mother amidst the Dagenham Girl Pipers during their visit to the show in the 1950s.

Sandringham church provides the backdrop for the Queen Mother's tour.

Mr Waite became a member of the flower show committee in 1967. He succeeded Horace Parsons as head gardener and as chairman of the show. Following his retirement he stepped down as chairman of the show committee in 1998 and on behalf of the committee, the Queen Mother presented him with a cheque in appreciation of his loyal service.

He has never tired of the show. "There is nothing quite like it. It's unique. It's like a garden party where you pay to go in.' The event had changed because people expected more. "We used to have King's Lynn Town Band or a similar band plus one other entertainment such as the Dagenham Girl Pipers who gave a half-hour display in front of Sandringham House. The Queen Mother would come out on the terrace to see them while the public watched from a roped-off area."

The Dagenham Girl Pipers appeared at the show in 1958 when Prince Charles and Princess Anne - then aged nine and seven - joined their grandmother at the show. That afternoon while a crowd of thousands watched a display of dancing, marching and counter-marching by the pipers in front of Sandringham House the Queen Mother and the royal youngsters went on to the west terrace to see

The Queen Mother and Mr Waite admire exhibits in the flower marquee.

the performance. Twice a footman and the Prince and Princess had to retrieve three of the Queen Mother's pets - two corgis and a dachshund - which tried to join in the highland dancing. Another year Melton Toy Soldiers Carnival Band gave a display in the gardens watched by the Queen Mother.

Over the last 30 years the show committee has invited leading military bands and developed main arena entertainment which has become a non-stop programme to maintain the interest of the crowds.

Mr Waite says that for many years attendance figures had remained at a steady figure of at least 15,000 though the biggest attendances were after the war, probably because people had been starved of entertainment. In 1952 and 1953 the annual attendance was 20,000, doubling the pre-war record of 10,000. Mr Waite has tried to foster a welcoming atmosphere for

Immaculate displays of vegetables in the marquee.

everyone taking part. "The horticulture firms have always felt part of the show and get a warm welcome from officials."

In the 1980s the committee realised the show's fund raising potential as a charity and became geared to maximising its donations. "We have always given money away but not the vast sums we do now. We enjoy putting on the show and giving visitors, including foreign tourists, a full day out and we feel we are doing good as well," Mr Waite says.

Over the many years he had escorted the Queen Mother round the show he has discovered her particular interests. "Her joy is spotting the names of prizewinners she knows. She is always very interested in the vegetables, especially the collections, and when she looks at the bakery and preserves she likes to ask about the jellies."

Mr Waite is proud of the standard of entries the show receives. "It is a high standard for a village show and has become a prestige occasion. The Queen Mother is kept informed of the sums of money raised by the show which are given to charity. And the day after the show she always wants to know what the attendance was."

SANDRINGHAM HOUSE GARDENS
Trees

One of the original ancient oaks.

Trees are a vital feature of the Sandringham landscape, both around the Estate and in the Gardens. Unlike some estates there has always been a policy of continuous planting and trees of all sizes and ages can be found throughout the grounds which surround the House. One of the oldest and tallest of these is the Wellingtonia or Big Tree (*Sequoiadendron giganteum*) from California with its massive buttressed trunk and thick, soft punchable bark. There are several examples here, one of which was presented by Princess Christian of Denmark in 1863, presumably to mark the marriage of Prince Albert Edward to Princess Alexandra in March of that year. It stands as a focal point at the junction of the Woodland Walk path and the re-aligned drive just east of the Old Father Time statue. The age of these Wellingtonias, however, pales into insignificance against two or three ancient, gnarled Oaks with their massive trunks – some rotten and hollow – one of which is reputed to be between 700 – 800 years old!

During the Victorian period,

planting of large conifers was popular, particularly where space was available as in many country houses. At Sandringham there are a number of examples, some of which have been planted as individual specimens such as the Cedar of Lebanon (*Cedrus libani*) while others like Austrian Pine (*Pinus nigra*) have been used more functionally to provide shelter and screening, particularly around the perimeter of the gardens. The range of trees in the gardens is great and includes some uncommon varieties and others which possess interesting features of flower, fruit and leaf. A typical example is the Handkerchief Tree (*Davidia involucrata*) which is located just inside the Woodland Walk on the west side of the Norwich Gates. It is fairly insignificant until its name is justified in the late spring or early summer when it produces small, rounded flowers enclosed by three enormous white bracts giving the tree an appearance of being covered in handkerchiefs.

One of the policies within the Gardens is to try and provide some interest at all times of the year, particularly when members of the Royal Family are in residence, and this is taken into account when selecting trees for planting. Late winter and spring are dominated by the blossoms of flowering Cherries (*Prunus spp.*) and Crab Apples (*Malus spp.*) and the beautiful newly emerging leaves of green, gold and purple on many other deciduous trees. Early summer sees Hawthorn (*Crataegus spp.*), Laburnum and Horse Chestnut (*Aesculus*) in flower. There is a good specimen of a rare form of the latter (*Aesculus x neglecta georgiana*) just south of the House which has smaller leaves than usual and orangey-red flower spikes.

Many trees provide high summer interest with their foliage, including some excellent examples of Maples (*Acer spp.*). There are two or three large specimens of Japanese Maple (*Acer palmatum and A.p. Atropurpureum*) at the north end of the upper lake and others can be found within the Woodland Walk such as Acer japonicum Laciniatum (an unusual form with cut leaves). Anyone exhibiting Bonsai in the pot-plant class of the flower show will find inspiration in these as well as the bright young pinky-cream leaves of the slow growing form of Sycamore (*Acer pseudoplatanus Brilliantissum*) to be found in several locations around the Woodland Walk and Long Border on the eastern boundary.

Autumn foliage colour can be found throughout the gardens; the coppery-gold of Beech, the brilliant red of Acer ginnala (another excellent Bonsai) at the bottom of the Stream Garden and the pale yellows of various Birches (*Betula spp.*). Several of these Birches also make excellent winter specimens because of their brilliant bark in silver (*Betula pendula*), cream (*Betula costata*) or pink-tinged (*Betula albo-sinensis Septentrionalis*).

A spectacular Blue Cedar.

Rose grower Peter Beales presents a new variety to the Queen Mother.

As the show chairman escorts the Queen Mother into the flower tent they are greeted by a spectacular display of 2000 magnificent roses. Peter Beales, the Attleborough rose specialist, is a regular exhibitor at Chelsea Flower Show, but he has a special affection for the Sandringham show where he has had a stand since 1970. "We treat it as one of our more important shows. We do not do a great deal of business but it is a prestige event for us," he says. "We put on the best show we can. We always enjoy ourselves - everyone is so friendly."

Mr Beales says the scene in the flower tent could be any village show around the country. It is not pretentious - but it is unique. "There is more to Sandringham because you rub shoulders with estate workers and royalty - the whole social strata," he says. Mr Beales likes the show for the way it stays the same. "The only changes are the roses we display. Our stand has been in the same place for 20 years which gives me a sense of *deja vu*. It is the only national show I know where there is no

The Queen Mother especially likes scented roses.

electricity on the site. On the eve of the show we have to arrange our display of 80 bowls each with 20 roses before it gets dark but we have sometimes had to finish the stand by the light of the car headlights."

Mr Beales says the Queen Mother is always interested in new roses. "Often the names of the other roses she knows catch her eye. She knows roses and loves them, especially old-fashioned roses which date back to the last century. I think she likes quieter colours and she likes perfume and asks if a rose is scented and then likes to smell it." Each year he presents a bloom of a new rose to the royal visitors. One year it was a rose named Royal Smile. "It was directly related to a royal smile we know so well. Once she spotted a particular rose and, with a twinkle in her eye, asked who had named it. The rose was called Sexy Rexy."

Mr Beales was invited to redesign and refurbish the rose garden at the Queen Mother's home at Royal Lodge, Windsor, as a present from the Prince of Wales for her 85th birthday. "We talk about it and she tells me it is looking nice. The Prince shares his grandmother's affection for roses. You can tell he grows them," Mr Beales says.

"When the royal party have left and the flower marquee opens to the public, thousands of people stream in. Hundreds of people who come from the Midlands in coaches ooh and aah at the roses because many of them don't even have gardens. They like to follow in the Queen Mother's footsteps and see what she has looked at. They want to know what she asked about and what is her favourite rose."

Most of the floral gifts are ferried to the royal cars but the Queen Mother likes to keep at least one rose in her hand and she occasionally pauses to appreciate its perfume. She is well aware of the sort of pictures press photographers hope to get and that they have a job to do and it is with the utmost co-operation that she happily poses with her favourite blooms.

Over the years other rose growers have given the Queen Mother examples of their prize blooms including Willem and Doris Tysterman of Wisbech Plant Company, Le Grice Roses of North Walsham and Fryers Nurseries of Knutsford, Cheshire.

The atmosphere in the flower tent is scent-laden and though some blooms - and humans - may wilt in the heat of a summer's day, the Queen Mother jauntily keeps walking, talking and smiling. She has followed the development and growth of the show with keen interest. The emphasis of the show remains with the 70 classes of flowers, fruit, vegetables and preserves which are only open to estate workers and pensioners, and tenants of estate cottages. There are 18 open amateur classes for floral art and flowers. She spends half an hour in the peace of the flower marquees before they are opened to the public so there is plenty of space for her to inspect the carefully-displayed individual entries in the cottagers' classes and she talks earnestly with the show chairman and the judges about the standard of the exhibits each year.

The number of cottagers' classes in each section has remained constant though the size of the entry in each class can vary from year to year according to weather conditions. There is always a varied display of cut flowers with roses, phlox, carnations, pinks, dahlias, antirrhinums, gladioli and sweet peas plus collections of annuals and perennials, and baskets of flowers creating a huge splash of colour. There are four classes for plants in pots including fuchsias and foliage plants.

Flower judge Brian Wild from Norwich has been officiating at Sandringham for 20 years and describes the show as "the highlight of my year". He enjoys its special atmosphere. "It is essentially a village show which makes no pretences to be anything else with the exhibits on trestle tables and the tent stakes knocked into the ground just like anywhere else. But everyone is made to feel very welcome and the pleasures of the show are very simple."

There are 25 cottagers' classes for vegetables which include potatoes, onions, shallots, peas, beans, marrows, cabbages, cauliflowers, carrots, turnips, lettuce and radishes. The collections of either six or nine vegetables carefully laid out on moss-lined trays are especially fascinating and always attract the attention of the royal party. There are nine classes for

The Prince of Wales among the flowers in the late 1980s.

Bakery and preserves judge Jean Thurston shows the Queen Mother exhibits under glass during a hot show day.

fruit including raspberries, gooseberries, currants including a collection of four kinds.

The mouth-watering bakery and preserves always catch the Queen Mother's eye. There are seven classes in each section. Competitors have to use the recipes provided for cheese scones, Victoria sandwich (recently changed from a sponge sandwich), fruit cake and gingerbread. They can chose their own recipes for Madeira cake, jam tarts and sausage rolls.

Strawberry, raspberry and blackcurrant jam feature in the preserves section along with marmalade, lemon curd, jelly and chutney.

Jean Thurston has cast an expert eye over the bakery and preserves at many Sandringham shows. She has seen bottled fruit, bread and wine disappear from the schedule of classes but Victoria sandwich, fruit cake and gingerbread maintain traditions in the cottagers' classes. Mrs Thurston has extensive experience as a judge and says the standard of entries is always good with exceptional skill displayed by some competitors. She thought the high standard was influenced by many competitors being WI members.

She first became involved in the mid-1960s when she was a rural domestic economy adviser for Norfolk County Council. Since those days she has seen few major changes in the show. "Its appeal is that it stays the same," she says.

Efforts have been made to encourage competitors by providing recipes with smaller quantities so limiting the cost and effort involved. "People can make a ginger cake and put it in a tin to mature. We have retained a class for fruit cake because men seem to like it and sometimes men enter them. We have introduced a special children's class for five butterfly cakes."

Preserves have been popular classes because cottagers grow soft fruit. They can now be exhibited in twist-top jars instead of the traditional wax top and cellophane which is a less effective seal. Another move with the times is the introduction of chutney.

Entries have to be delivered to the marquees on the eve of the show and Mrs Thurston and her fellow judge, Eleanor Pearson of Luton, wearing their crisp white overalls, begin judging at 8am on show day so they have completed their task before the royal visit. "It's a pleasure to see everything so beautifully presented for judging. It is all under perspex - it used to be under glass. People love to see the exhibits," Mrs Thurston says.

Royal visitors share the enthusiasm. "The Queen Mother is very enthusiastic and is pleased that people still do this sort of baking. She is also very interested in the jellies. The Prince of Wales is most interested and says he likes foods in their season - and he obviously likes fruit cake. He likes to know who has won because he is familiar with the names of people living on the estate."

Mrs Pearson, a national judge, has teamed up with Mrs Thurston to judge at Sandringham for 20 years. "The show is unique," she says. "There is no other village show quite like it." She describes the Queen Mother as amazing and admires her knowledge of cookery and preserves and thinks her love of jellies has influenced their inclusion in the preserves section. After the Queen Mother has had a good chat with the two judges Prince Charles joins them for a discussion about the exhibits. "Their interest is very genuine and they almost thank us for coming. Everyone makes us very welcome."

SANDRINGHAM HOUSE GARDENS
Garden Maintenance

The Pleached Lime Avenue needs regular maintenance.

The Gardens at Sandringham are planted and maintained on a week to week, and year to year basis very much along the lines of most small domestic gardens. One policy followed on the Estate which can be applied to gardens of any size, is that plants are selected to suit the prevailing conditions, whether wet or dry, sunny or shady, acid or alkaline.

Wet areas around the lakes and stream are therefore planted with appropriate bog garden plants such as Astilbe, Rodgersia, Iris – while dry shady areas found below and around the larger trees in the Dell and Woodland Walk are covered in Periwinkle (*Vinca minor*) or Oregon Grape (*Mahonia aquifolium*). The only exceptions to this policy are the ericaceous plants, particularly the bed of Japanese Azaleas in the Dell which makes a spectacular display of pink, red and yellow flowers in spring.

The soil is very free draining sand with a neutral pH – a combination of conditions which can lead to yellowing of the leaves (chlorosis) and stress, resulting in weak plants. To try and improve the situation, a regular acidifying mulch of pine needles is applied in late winter. Irrigation is only used on newly planted areas until plants are reasonably established, and are then left to fend for themselves. Experience has shown that excessive watering can lead to shallow root systems which are more vulnerable to drought. Mulching with products from the Estate, such as pine needles, and chipped waste wood or bark as a by-product of the forestry operations, is carried out in most areas of ornamental planting.

In the 'wilder' or less-managed areas of the gardens, fallen leaves from the various woodland trees are left in-situ as a natural mulch. Pruning and management of both woody and perennial plants follows exactly the same lines as in any small garden – only the scale is different. Some earlier plantings have now matured to a stage where major cutting back is needed either to rejuvenate the plants themselves or to open up views and vistas which have become obscured. Dwarf conifers can create problems if allowed to grow into each other. Foliage die-back occurs which will not usually regenerate, leaving bare, brown patches. Thinning out or trimming back before this situation can arise is followed as far as possible, particularly on the Upper Lake Rockery and above the waterfall to the lower lake which is densely planted with such conifers.

Pruning tends to be limited to plants, such as the conifers, which will suffer or deteriorate if not looked after. Buddleia, Lavender and Potentilla varieties are mostly trimmed to keep them bushy and encourage better flowering. Formative pruning, merely to improve the shape of wayward plants is less of a priority. The main exception is the annual pruning and training of the Pleached Lime Avenue along the North Garden and cutting the box hedges and yew hedges in front of the eastern entrance to the House.

Areas of formal, annual bedding are very small and are chiefly confined to stone urns and containers used as hot-spots and a narrow bed immediately around the house. The labour intensive nature of such planting is one reason for its limited use, but equally relevant has been the wishes of successive occupants of the house, dating right back to Edward, Prince of Wales and Princess Alexandra, to retain the predominantly informal nature of the grounds. As part of this policy the original formal parterres and traditional herbaceous borders to the west of the house have now been replaced with simple lawn and more easily managed shrub beds.

Making sure plants stay healthy.

The royal party concludes its tour of the marquees with a look at the dozens of entries in the highly popular open amateur classes including the immaculate floral art arrangements. The visitors also admire the great banks of flowers on the trade stands featuring specialities including lavender, fuchsias, clematis, delphiniums and alstroemerias. As she steps out of the tent into the sunshine the Queen Mother often receives the most vociferous welcome of the day as she is greeted with cheers and applause, a sea of smiling faces, clicking cameras and dozens of proferred gifts of flowers - and often the singing of Happy Birthday.

The welcome was never warmer than at the centenary show in 1980 which was like a giant birthday party for the Queen Mother from the moment the Band of the Royal Marines struck up Happy Birthday and set the theme for the day. It was echoed by a non-stop chorus which accompanied her two-hour tour. The enthusiasm and warmth of the crowd was almost overwhelming and the Queen Mother responded by spending longer than usual at the show chatting to dozens of people among the crowd, often standing ten-deep, lining her route. There was a big welcome, too, for the Duke and Duchess of Kent who stopped to talk to many spectators. With them was their younger son, Lord Nicholas Windsor, then aged 10.

The next year the show was cancelled because the date clashed with the wedding of the Prince of Wales and Lady Diana Spencer, so it was with renewed energy and enthusiasm that organisers staged the 101st show in 1982. Cheering and applause began the minute the royal party arrived. With the Duke and Duchess of Kent on that occasion was Lord Nicholas and the couple's 18-year-old daughter Lady Helen Windsor.

The excitement of seeing the Queen Mother and exchanging a few words with her often proves very emotional for some visitors to the show, especially pensioners who remember the role the King and Queen played in boosting the morale of the nation during the war years, and they are often moved to tears when they have come face to face with the royal favourite.

The Prince of Wales first went to the show as a child with Princess Anne and had never been back until 1985 when he put in a surprise appearance. "There's Charles!" was the delighted cry when he was spotted by people in the crowd. Prince Charles had arrived with his grandmother in an open carriage drawn by greys from the Royal Mews at Buckingham Palace. He clearly enjoyed his first real taste of the unique atmosphere of the show and quickly slipped into the royal routine - smelling the fragrance of roses, buying cakes from the WI, and then a basket in which he rather self-consciously carried his purchases.

Three years later he was back again to another big welcome, but he still ensured the day belonged to his grandmother and happily played a supporting role as the Queen Mother led the way round the showground. He obviously appreciated the informality of the occcasion and the opportunity to chat to horticulturalists about a subject close to his

Spectators are keen to photograph the Prince of Wales.

heart and to meet an admiring public. He told show chairman Fred Waite: "I would like to come every year." And he has.

The Prince has slipped into a pattern of joining his grandmother, usually flying to Sandringham on the eve of the show and often dashing off early the following day to fulfil other engagements.

Sir Hugh Casson, former president of the Royal Academy, has been a regular guest of the Queen Mother at the show. The WI modestly advertise their very popular raffle.

The Queen Mother is president of Sandringham Women's Institute and the flower show is one of the two highlights of the year for members. The other is their January meeting which is attended by the Queen Mother and the Queen who is also a WI member. During her tour of the show the Queen Mother always calls at the marquee run by Sandringham WI, which was formed in 1918 and first had a stall at the flower show in 1926. By 1931 they had their own tent selling hand-made crafts.

The Queen Mother usually makes several purchases and there is speculation about what happens to the many matinee coats, pairs of bootees, covered coat hangers and sweaters she has bought over the years. There was a broad hint in 1962 when she bought a yellow and white nylon toy rabbit and said: "Don't you think this would be lovely for Margaret's baby?"(Princess Margaret's son Viscount Linley). She once bought an apron for Princess Anne.

In the 1970s her purchases included blue velvet coathangers, a pink knitted shawl, a green wool pullover, and a jar of marmalade. In

The Duke of Kent watches as the Duchess of Kent and the Queen Mother make purchases in the WI tent.

1985 the Prince of Wales bought a baby's knitted cardigan and a fruit cake. Equerries pay for their purchases.

The royal association guarantees huge public support for the WI at the show, especially as the Queen and the Queen Mother give a raffle prize each year - a fact advertised modestly on the outside of the marquee. People queue to buy tickets which give them the chance of winning china, glassware, table mats or a tray from one of the royal residences. When the Prince of Wales started visiting the show he offered to donate a prize and his contributions have included a book and table mats illustrated with his paintings.

WI members used to spend many hours making baby clothes as well as household items such as hot water bottle covers and peg bags for sale at the show, but the demand for such crafts has waned while the demand for cakes and preserves has grown dramatically. So now members make just as many cakes as they can plus small packs of shortbread, scones and sausage rolls - all of which sell, literally, like hot cakes - and always earn admiring looks and comments from the royal party.

Meeting the people.

Gifts for Britain's favourite great-grandmother.

The Queen Mother always gets a big welcome and lots of gifts.

When she emerges from the WI marquee the Queen Mother embarks on an extensive walkabout. She covers a total of about half a mile from her arrival point at the show to the distant spot where she returns to her transport for the day. Spectators admired her stamina in 1975, as she approached her 75th birthday, when she spent well over an hour touring the show on a day which was so hot that the sides of marquees were lowered to allow more air to circulate.

Two years later when the Queen was celebrating her silver jubilee especially big crowds attended royal occasions and the flower show was no exception. Spectators stood 15 deep in places to cheer the Queen Mother and the Duke and Duchess of Kent who spent 90 minutes at the show. By the time the Queen Mother was nearly 80 there was even greater admiration for the stalwart way she way she toured the show for two hours - even longer than usual - clearly enjoying every moment. Her indomitable spirit prevailed as the Queen Mother strode through her eighties, maintaining a pace envied by people many years her junior.

Her 90th birthday passed and the ever-smiling Queen Mother did nothing to curtail the length of her visits, although her mobility began to be affected by a painful hip and she starting using a specially strengthened umbrella to give her extra support. A royal car was surreptitiously parked at a strategic point along the route of her walkabout and she was given the option of curtailing her long walk - still in her high heels - on the rough grass. But she always declined, not wanting to miss anything nor to disappoint stand-holders and spectators looking foward to welcoming her. The Queen Mother tried to make light of her deteriorating mobility as she bravely continued her visits using an elegant silver-topped stick. Her discomfort was etched in her face and it became clear she was also experiencing sight problems due to a cataract - but her enthusiasm never flagged for one moment.

Less than a week before the 1995 show the Queen Mother underwent an operation on a cataract affecting her left eye and there was apprehension that she would have to miss the event. But then she has never let physical ailments daunt her spirit and she arrived at the show as usual, obviously benefiting from improved vision. For the first time in public she used an electric golf buggy which enabled her to enjoy the show by giving relief to her painful hip. It was in great contrast to the open horse-drawn carriage in which the Queen Mother and the Prince of Wales travelled to and from the show.

In her own inimitable style the Queen Mother

Children say it with flowers.

The royal buggy - painted in her racing colours - does not stop the Queen Mother from meeting an admiring public.

treated her novel mode of transport as a new adventure playfully waving the Prince of Wales out of the way when she thought his toes were in danger of being run over by the buggy's wheels. Her walkabout became a ride-about as the buggy, driven by an equerry, zig-zagged along the roped-off pathway accepting greetings and flowers from the crowds on either side. She still stopped at marquees along the route to pay her usual visit to charities and organisations. Soon the space at the rear of the buggy designed to carry golf clubs was filled with dozens of posies, gifts and cards.

In November 1995 the Queen Mother underwent a hip replacement operation and a month later made her first public appearance when she attended church at Sandringham with other members of the Royal

The Queen Mother on her walkabout.

Family. In 1996 she was clearly enjoying the benefits of the surgery which had given her renewed energy and in 1997 spent nearly two hours at the show - her longest visit. Although she still carried her stick for reassurance she demonstrated the benefits of her hip replacement by spending more than 90 minutes walking round the showground - to the amazement of her admirers. Her buggy was on hand but she used it only for two brief rides when she was driven by her chauffeur in his uniform and peaked cap.

The Queen Mother's abiding interest in horse racing - and her sense of humour - are reflected in the way the buggy was painted in her racing colours of pale blue and old gold and carried her royal crest. By 1998 the livery had been completed with a black roof edged in gold to match the jockey's silks.

The crowds continued to marvel at the Queen Mother's stamina that she should spend a record two hours at the show which, she remarked, "gets better and better."

Stephen Pocklington, head of Sandringham and West Newton School, helps youngsters prepare work for the schools' tent.

One of the original aims of the show was to improve standards of writing and needlework among children living on the estate and to this end the schools in the area exhibited youngsters' work. Reports of the first shows refer to work which "showed genius as well as unflagging industry" and in 1922 there was reference to the "most meritorious exhibits of the handiwork of children attending the schools of Anmer, Dersingham, Flitcham, Sherbourne, West Newton and Wolferton".

In 1955 six schools on the estate contributed to displays of handwriting, needlework, woodwork and painting which were all admired by the Queen Mother. The next year she commented on the variety of styles of handwriting from Great Bircham School where the children of Air Force personnel were among the pupils. She also praised the standard of dresses made by girls aged 13-15 at Dersingham Secondary Modern School and the canvas woodwork of boys from Dersingham Primary School. She showed a keen interest in an oak upholstered piano stool made by 15-year-old Terence Finbow from Dersingham. In 1965, when four schools participated, the Queen Mother plucked the strings of a guitar which was among the crafts made by boys at Dersingham. The next year she strummed the guitar made by Richard Fanneran of Harpley which won first prize.

There was no school tent in 1968 because the schools had been closed for two weeks before the show on July 31 and it was felt that displays did not adequately represent the work done by pupils at that time. But schools' participation in the show resumed after Stephen Pocklington was appointed head teacher at Sandringham and West Newton School and he was asked to revive the schools tent. Since the 1980s Sandringham, Flitcham and Ingoldisthorpe primary schools, and occasionally St George's, Dersingham, have contributed to a joint display.

Mr Pocklington did not reintroduce the competitions which were previously featured but instead has filled the tent with what he describes as "an Aladdin's cave" full of colourful displays to which almost all pupils contribute. "I think it looks more exciting with everything squeezed in," he says. Sometimes they have a theme such as when the tent had a party atmosphere for the Queen Mother's 90th birthday - including a table set with papier mâché food including cakes and blancmange. If there is no specific theme, the schools look at work they have done during the past year and chose projects which are visually most interesting such as records of Sandringham school's annual week-long stay in Derbyshire. "The Queen Mother and the Prince of Wales display a very genuine interest and often spend nearly half an hour with us," Mr Pocklington says.

A touch of humour in the schools' tent.

SANDRINGHAM HOUSE GARDENS
Flower Arranging

The floral art classes at the flower show, especially the open amateur classes, attract dozens of competitors who need a ready supply of flowers and foliage. Anyone with an interest in flower arranging will be inspired by the range of hardy plants suitable for cutting and arranging to be found within Sandringham Gardens.

The plants have not been selected as material for arrangements but for their qualities of flower, foliage and habit which contribute to the overall effect in the Gardens. The choice of plants means there is something of interest at any time of the year - and that is good news for a floral artist.

In the depths of winter flowering shrubs are very welcome. Mahonia (*Mahonia* Charity) is a traditional plant for this time of year. Less frequently grown, however, is Winter Sweet (*Chimonanthus praecox*) which has beautiful, scented purple-centred yellow flowers on bare stems in January and February. Normally it requires the protection of a south or west facing wall but in the Gardens it is sheltered by surrounding trees and shrubs in the Woodland Walk. Plants with coloured or interesting stems are also worthwhile in winter when flowers in the garden may be scarce. The red and green stems of Dogwood (*Cornus spp.*) are well known for this reason. Less well-known, but equally striking, is a particular Willow (*Salix fargesii*) to be found at the lower end of the Stream Walk. The one or two year old stems of this large shrub are a dark shining brown and this makes the large, bright red winter buds even more conspicuous.

Evergreens, whether shrubs, conifers or

Shrubs and perennials also provide the raw material for floral arts.

SANDRINGHAM HOUSE GARDENS

perennials are indispensable to floral artists, and the grounds contain many examples of popular varieties such as Elaeagnus pungens Maculata, Hollies (*Ilex spp.*) and both green and golden forms of Yew (*Taxus baccata spp.*). Plants with spiky or sword-shaped leaves lend themselves very well to arranging, and at the eastern end of the Woodland Walk there is a trio of large New Zealand Flax (*Phormium tenax; P.t. Variegatum* and *P.t. Purpureum*). At first this group seems slightly incongruous, but when seen in full sun with a Silver Willow leaved Pear (*Pyrus salicifolia Pendula*) and Blue Cedar (*Cedrus atlantica Glauca*) behind, the combination takes on a Mediterranean feel. Autumn fruits, berries and seeds give an extra dimension to arranging and traditional plants for this purpose like Firethorn (*Pyracantha* Orange Glow) and female Hollies (*Ilex aquifolium* Golden King) for example, are to be found in several areas.

Just above the upper lake can be found a less well–known shrub, the Bladder Nut (*Staphylea colchica*). Relatively inconspicuous for most of the year, its clusters of green and white flowers in late spring produce amazing inflated pods like large translucent-white Chinese lanterns later in the year. The margins of the two lakes and the stream are rich in plants suited to floral art. Many of these are very popular, including Hosta (*H. fortunei Albomarginata* and *H. undulata Erromena*), Primula (*P. pulverulenta*), *Ligularia dentata* Desdemona, Astilbe in variety and Iris (*I. laevigata* Rose Queen, I. sibirica) to name but a few.

Formal plantings of Floribunda and Hybrid Tea Roses are surprisingly very limited, confined mostly to small groups of such varieties as Wembley Stadium, Arthur Bell, Mountbatten and Helga within the rectangular and square borders of the North Garden. Planted alongside these Roses are other suitable plants such as Penstemon (P. Sour Grapes, Alice Hindley, Preston Hall), Thalictrum and Centaurea pulchra Major all of which are enclosed by formal hedges of Box (*Buxus sempervirens*) itself an excellent subject.

A useful herbaceous border for a flower arranger.

The Queen sees entries in the fur and feather section run for 50 years by Arthur Hammond Browne (centre).

It was thanks to the generosity of a West Norfolk newsagent that the flower show featured a fur and feather section for 50 years. Arthur Hammond Browne took just one day's holiday a year to run the highly popular and successful section, bearing many of the costs himself. The businessman, an expert on exhibition poultry, approached the show committee in 1934 and asked if he could run a fur and feather section in conjunction with the show.

His request was accepted and he established a marquee featuring dozens of classes for poultry, pigeons, rabbits, cavies, cage birds and eggs which became a popular feature of the show and went from strength to strength. A typical show featured some 270 rabbits, 120 pigeons and 100 cage birds with entries coming from as far away as Scotland and Wales. By the 1960s the budgerigar entry hit a record and there were 230 pigeons entered, including the Queen's racing pigeons.

The show continued to break its own records and by 1968 Mr Hammond Browne had to turn away

The Queen and Queen Mother, dressed for the rain at the 1974 show, tour the fur and feather tent.

entries because he did not have enough cages. People from all over the British Isles wanted to take part with hundreds of canaries, pigeons and rabbits on show although poultry numbers did drop. As in the flower tent, a win in the fur and feather section at Sandringham was regarded as a great honour by fanciers.

Len Rush of King's Lynn, who became the Queen's racing pigeon manager in 1962, entered her birds in some of the 40 classes and they regularly won prizes. She used to visit the Royal Lofts in the back garden of Mr Rush s semi-detached house at Gaywood. In 1970 the Queen Mother saw six of her homing birds, called Liberty birds, at the show. They normally had freedom of flight in Windsor Great Park.

More records were broken in 1975 when nearly 1000 birds were entered and judges reported high quality and the pigeon class, which had 300 entries, was given championship status. By then there were about 70 classes for rabbits, 40 for poultry and 30 for cavies.

The Queen Mother watches judging of the fur and feather show.

The highlight of the Queen Mother's visit to Sandringham Fur and Feather Society's 40th show in 1977 was when she saw for the first time Buff Orpington poultry presented to her in the centenary year of the Poultry Club of Great Britain. The poultry won two first prizes and Mr Hammond Browne, who was president of the National Buff Orpington Club, kept the Buff Orpingtons for the Queen Mother to breed from them.

In 1979 Lord Nicholas Windsor, younger son of the Duke and Duchess of Kent, who was celebrating his ninth birthday on the day of the show, was intrigued by rabbits he saw being judged and asked if he could have one. An exhibitor learned of his

Eleven-year-old Lady Diana Spencer with her guinea pig Peanuts.

request and gave Lord Nicholas a black and white Dutch rabbit which the youngster said he would call Arthur and which he took home in a cardboard box.

The most famous competitor in the fur and feather section was to be a shy 11-year-old girl. She was spotted by EDP photographer John Hocknell who took what was to become a classic picture of Lady Diana Spencer with her guinea pig Peanuts which won the pets class. There was an amusing sequel to the photo for a few weeks later Mr Hammond Browne received a phone call from Lady Diana's home at Park House, Sandringham, pointing out that she had not yet received her silver cup or her half crown prize.

The royal visitors are always pleased to buy a shopping basket. The Queen Mother makes her choice.

The Prince of Wales looks a little self-conscious with his.

About half way along the route of the walkabout the royal party is always glad when marquees occupied by Norfolk and Norwich Association for the Blind and the Red Cross come into view for they sell baskets which prove very useful for carrying their purchases. Sometimes when the Queen Mother has been almost swamped with cards and gifts her equerry Sir Ralph Anstruther would hurry ahead to buy a shopping basket. Both charities have had a presence at the show for years and welcome the interest and support of members of the Royal Family whose visits raise the profile of each organisation's work.

"The Queen Mother always comes to see us and we look forward to seeing who she brings with her. It has been especially nice to see the Queen and the

The Duchess of Kent shows the Queen Mother her purchases.

Prince of Wales," says administrator Julie Lythgoe. The organisation used to have workshops where baskets and mats were made for sale and socks made in London were popular. The Queen Mother has bought many baskets and she speaks to staff and volunteers in the tent as well as blind people who are sometimes working on crafts. "It's wonderful and gives us all a boost," Mrs Lythgoe says. The Queen Mother has bought many pairs of socks over the years. In 1957 she bought a dozen pairs as well as a twin set and a cane basket. Seven years later she bought another dozen pairs of socks, five wicker shopping baskets and a toast rack. In 1970 she bought two bristle scrubbing brushes.

Elizabeth McKechnie of the Red Cross says the show provided a very good outlet for the sale of crafts

SANDRINGHAM HOUSE GARDENS
Judging

Four pairs of judges use their expertise to assess exhibits in the flower show. One pair marking the fruit and vegetable classes together with the cottagers' gardens belonging to workers on the Sandringham Estate and retired workers and tenants. Entries come from Sandringham and nearby villages and are judged a month before the show.

Although there is plenty of friendly rivalry and competition between the entrants for this class, it is perhaps not quite so intense as in the past when there were more competitors and fewer alternative spare time interests. The criteria for judging these gardens are based on the Royal Horticultural Society's rules for allotments and gardens. They award points for different aspects such as overall appearance and layout, general husbandry, cleanliness and hygiene, and crop rotation as well as the quality of produce grown in the garden, notably fruit and vegetables. A degree of flexibility has to be applied since the size of the gardens can vary considerably, as indeed can the age of the gardeners themselves.

At the end of the day, where there is any cause for doubt in the application of the RHS rules, the judges call on their own experience and knowledge to make a decision. The overall winner of the cottagers' gardens class can look forward to receiving the King George VI silver cup presented by the president at the luncheon on the day of the show. Judging the marquee exhibits is quite an exhausting process because there may be literally hundreds of entries spread through 90 classes and awards have to be made and put in place before The Queen Mother's tour starts. Some classes are arguably more straightforward to judge, particularly in the vegetable sections where the judges are able to compare like with like within any particular class such as potatoes or tomatoes, and can refer to well-defined and recognised criteria for awarding points to decide the winners and runners-up. However, there are other classes such as pot plants and flower arts where the criteria are somewhat looser and more open to personal interpretation by the judges because no two arrangements are be the same.

Awards down to fourth and fifth can be made and the judges often find these places are the hardest to decide as the general standard throughout is so high. This is where the judges discretion comes into play and they may therefore make a decision in favour of one plant over another because of its rarity value or because it might require greater skill to cultivate successfully.

Finally, judging of the Sandringham Flower Show is apparently not for the unfit. Conditions inside marquees full of plants on a hot July day can be very humid and racing up and down several hundred feet of display benches for two to three hours must be something akin to running a horticultural marathon.

Les Secker

Les Secker has been interested in gardening since he was 16 "Although these days I'm considered to be a bit of an all-rounder, in the past I've specialised in several flowering subjects including Carnations, Roses and Sweet Peas. My interest in fruit and vegetables was, a spin-off from these."

Mr Secker judged his first flower show when he was only 23, more than 50 years ago, and has travelled all over Norfolk and Suffolk using his expertise. Among his horticultural achievements he is particularly proud of two Dahlias which he raised himself. "I put forward Dahlia Aztec Gold for trial with the National Dahlia Society in 1987 and was very pleased when it was awarded a bronze medal. Another of my Dahlia introductions was named Amanda Dawn after my grand-daughter, who is carrying on the family interest in plants with her flower shop at Dereham."

Mr Secker has been involved with the Sandringham Flower Show for several years. "I was fortunate enough to be included in the Royal Horticultural Society national register of show judges. That, together with a recommendation at the time by an existing judge, began my association with Sandringham."

Brian Wild

Brian Wild's liking for plants goes back more than 30 years, when he looked after two allotments. "My first love was really vegetables which I grew to exhibition standard, but subsequently I became very interested in plants of a more ornamental nature including Fuchsias, Chrysanthemums and Sweet Peas."

Mr Wild was secretary of the Thorpe and District Gardening Club at Norwich for 23 years, looking after their annual show and other events. "I was also a member of the Norfolk and Norwich Horticultural Society, exhibited at the Royal Norfolk show, and became show secretary for seven years."

He has judged shows all over Norfolk for 20 years, and has been a judge at Sandringham for more than half that period. "I took early retirement after 40 years working on the railways – now as well as my role as a judge, I write articles for magazines and give talks. The organisation behind Sandringham Flower Show is excellent, and the standard of exhibits particularly floral and fruit has continued to improve during my association with it."

The Prince of Wales meets the men of the Suffolk and Norfolk Yeomanry.

made by disabled people. "The Queen Mother always asks about our work and is concerned about how we are doing and often buys a basket or a tray," she says. In 1955 the Queen Mother named a new British Red Cross mobile hospital in front of 1200 officers, members and cadets. The next year the facility was used to treat nearly 100 minor casualities at the show including cuts, stings and grazes.

The British Legion and St Raphael Clubs are among other charities which have taken part in the show and where the Queen Mother has bought items ranging from a toy wooden Dalmatian to a fruit bowl and Christmas cards. She often chatted to St Raphael Club member Gill Shaw of King's Lynn who usually had her pet corgis with her.

The beekeepers tent – for those with a sweet tooth.

King Edward VII, who as Prince of Wales was an enthusiastic patron of the flower show from its beginnings in 1866, formed the King's Own Imperial Norfolk Yeomanry in 1902, the year after he ascended the throne. The Yeomanry has a distinguished history and amalgamated with the Suffolk Yeomanry in 1960 to form the Suffolk and Norfolk Yeomanry which has had a display at the flower show for many years. Its territorial soldiers welcome royal attention and show the Queen Mother their weaponry and regimental silver. Former Battery Commander, Major Gary Walker, says the Queen Mother was always interested in their activities and training and liked to see the special selection of silver.

Members of the royal party are always invited to sign the visitors' book, but that caused a problem for the Prince of Wales in 1990 when he was suffering from a broken arm following a fall while playing polo. His right arm was in a sling under his jacket so he had to sign with his left hand, joking that he had been practising the signature throughout the previous evening.

King's Lynn and District Beekeepers Association is a popular destination for the Queen Mother and her guests who always spend some minutes admiring the dozens of jars of different honeys entered in the organisation's main event of the year. The beekeepers

Are they all for me?

returned to the show in 1968 after a gap of 15 years and since then have expanded from a stall in the flower tent to having their own marquee.

Show secretary Pam Rix says that although there was a decreasing number of people who kept bees there was always great interest in the honey show. The Queen Mother and the Prince of Wales were each given a prize-winning jar of honey and both were always keen to see the exhibits and to watch the bees working in an observation hive. She says members of the royal party bought honey and honeycomb and were very good customers for beeswax furniture polish for their antiques. Some of the trophies competed for at the show were given by the Queen Mother's close friend Ruth, Lady Fermoy.

Since the early 1980s the last call has been on the Sandringham Association of Royal Warrant Holders which makes the show a family day for its 160 members. They are mainly from East Anglia and provide a wide variety of goods and services to the Royal Family at Sandringham ranging from meat and potatoes to bulbs, tractors and gamekeepers'

Time to go home...

uniforms. The association presents both the Queen Mother and the Prince of Wales with a large basket of strawberries.

A Sandringham cricket team always has a match on the ground in the park on show day and in recent years has been challenged by the Royal Warrant Holders for the Aubrey Aitken Cup.

As the royal visit nears its end between 12.30 and 1pm crowds drift away from the route of the walkabout to see for themselves all the attractions enjoyed by the Queen Mother. But first, thousands settle themselves on the grass to picnic to the accompaniment of music by Springwood High School Concert Band from King's Lynn while, in the main arena, a four-hour programme of entertainment gets under way. It caters for a wide range of interests and has included freefall parachutists, aerobatic displays, historic vehicles, shire horses, falconry, mounted games, model aeroplanes, sheepdogs, veteran cyclists, carriage driving and archery. Leading gundog handlers are invited by the estate's head gamekeeper to take part in trials introduced to the show in 1968 and which continue to be a popular feature.

The Church of St Mary Magdalene, where the Royal Family worship when they stay on the estate, is open on show day and visitors queue to see inside, just as they did at the first shows well over a century ago. It is just one of the traditions which the show organisers want to retain. The chairman, Chief Superintendent David Reeve, says the committee carefully considers any proposed changes to the format of the day. "The show is unique and has tremendous tradition which we want to maintain and a careful balance has to be measured when we discuss new ventures. We receive applications from thousands of people wanting to take part but we must keep standards high. We want quality and variety. The show stands apart because it has retained its composure with a blend of tradition and quality. It has a following which is unprecedented - generations of families have visited over the years."

Mr Reeve became a member of the committee because, as head of royal security in Norfolk, he is closely involved with the police operation at the show which is geared to its traditions and informality while also providing appropriate security. An example is the popular practice of people in the crowd presenting flowers to the Queen Mother which has led to the familiar sight of police officers assisting with carrying the hundreds of posies. "As chairman my role is to carry on very much in the traditional way, honouring traditional values and ensuring the show retains its popularity," Mr Reeve says.

The committee members are guardians of the show who carefully protect its uniqueness. All their energies are devoted to one day in the year when they are responsible for staging an event which is dignified yet informal. But they are also very conscious that they provide the setting for one of the Queen Mother's most cherished public appearances of the year - and one which has gained even greater significance as each year has passed.

In terms of royal walkabouts the Queen Mother's tour of the show is a marathon which is in a class of its own. Her visit has almost ritual qualities but it is not prescribed and timed to the minute like official public engagements. At the show the Queen Mother can, and does, chat to whoever she likes for as long as she likes. That she never seems in any hurry is a very public statement of how much she enjoys herself.

Thousands throng the area where the royal visit ends as the Queen Mother, still smiling and waving, makes her farewells. The show always epitomises her *'joie de vivre'*, her warmth, sincerity, her interest in people and her exceptional memory for faces and names. Her enduring affection for the show is reflected in the length of her visits which have got longer rather than shorter. As she says her goodbyes to the chairman and Queen's agent she offers words of great praise for the show and expresses her continuing delight in her annual visit. She comments on how successful it is, how it continues to grow - and that she wouldn't want to miss it.

Sandringham Church fascinates visitors.

Thank you for a lovely day!